Other books by Author

... more will be revealed soon...

Other books by Author

... more will be revealed soon...

WAR WITHIN

WW I:
BATTLE OF THE MIND

VOLUME 1 OF 7

MICHAEL R. BANE

WESTBOW
PRESS®
A DIVISION OF THOMAS NELSON
& ZONDERVAN

WestBow Press books may be ordered through booksellers or by contacting:

WestBow Press
A Division of Thomas Nelson & Zondervan
1663 Liberty Drive
Bloomington, IN 47403
www.westbowpress.com
844-714-3454

All Scripture quotations are taken from the King James Version.

ISBN: 978-1-6642-3451-2 (sc)
ISBN: 978-1-6642-3450-5 (e)

Print information available on the last page.

WestBow Press rev. date: 06/22/2021

CONTENTS

Chapter 1   My Pen

Chapter 2   Angels, and Demons

Chapter 3   Warfare

Chapter 4   Masks

Chapter 5   Pain

Chapter 6   Living Water

Chapter 7   Love

DEDICATION

I dedicate this book to my Father, John Bane Sr. He is the greatest man I know. He was my hero, and taught me so many things.

We shared some of the same battles.

We fought many of the same demons.

There was many struggles along the journey.

But we also shared many of the same victories.

I do know that their is a war within that will never cease, until we see God; face to face.

I love you Dad, and I miss you.

Thank - you for ...
Everything.

Exodus 20:12

Honour thy Father and thy mother: that thy days may be long
upon the land which the Lord thy God giveth thee.

INTRODUCTION/ABOUT THE AUTHOR

Those are poems, thoughts, and ideals from the heart, mind, and spirit of Michael Bane.
Many of my life experiences, as well as those who may have had similar experiences in their own lives are expressed here.
My hopes for this edition, are that I may connect with others who may feel some of the things, I feel.
And even bigger, that we would all connect with God on new levels.
In some of the darkest times in my life, God showed up, and the will for you also.

* All bible verses - KJV -

CHAPTER 1

MY PEN

Exodus 34:27a

And the Lord said unto Moses
Write thou, these words

KJV

WHEN IT WAS WRITTEN

MY PEN

I love it when my pen just flows
it knows exactly where to go
and on the page I bare my soul
at times like Edgar Allen Poe

My pen can be a friend, or foe
at times from above
but others below

I read the story
as it unfolds

It just won't stop
it grows and grows
its spreads its wings
the ink I throw

at times I think
it might explode.

I never find a dead end road
this story of mine
it must be told.

and on the page
I bare my soul
my pen, in hand

where will it stop?
where will it go?
there's times that even I don't know.

A LETTER

If my life was a letter
that anyone could read
by simply looking at me.

How would this letter read?
If anyone could see
and simply watch me

things that are not
written on paper
or even etched in stone

But the things that I do
on a daily basis
if anyone could see this.

Now how would it read?
Not with ink, or words
But with God's loving spirit

If my life was a letter
Is it something, that even
I would want to read?

I BELONG

I sometimes worry that
I don't know where to go
Not sure where I belong

I sometimes worry that
I'm a mistake
I'm doing wrong

I sometimes worry that
I won't last
that this life is too long

I sometimes worry that
I am weak, but I remember
He is strong

I sometimes worry
then I remember
to whom, I belong

THIS INK

I take a journey through my mind
So many, many memories
are there to find.

To some I run to
From others I flee
I want to use my experiences
to help someone like me.

I want to change this world
With my paper, and my pen
So this ink spills
From many places I have been.

There are times I don't
wanna do this anymore
but I put my pen to paper
and I'm not sure
who it's for.

If I stop writing
I may just die
So the truth must be told
to defeat the lie.

That you are not worth it
I'm here to say you are
and so am I.

So this ink continues to flow
Is it for you,
or is it for me?
Only the ink knows.

I WRITE

When I sit alone at night
I search my mind, and then I write
I write about the things I feel
I write about me
things that are real
things that I see.
I pour my heart out on the page
and this is just another stage
of who I am, what I've became.
I write about my thoughts, my dreams
I write about my private things
things I choose to share with you
things I think, things I do.
and as I write, I also feel
this is me, this is real...

THIS ARMOR

One of those days
became one of those years.
I woke up today
listening to your lies
trying to spread your fear.
this is war, but
the battle is not real.
It's just another
one of those days,
that became another
one of those years,
Although it may seem different
its really not.
It was all written
you cannot penetrate
this Armor...
spew your lies
spread your fear
I woke up today
ready for you...

CHAPTER 2

ANGELS, AND DEMONS

Proverbs 30:5

Every word of God is pure
He is a shield unto them,
that put their trust in Him

KJV

WHEN IT WAS WRITTEN

WATCH ME BURN

So glad I didn't get
what I deserve

Grace, the favor
I didn't earn

Because, the enemy
He wants to watch me burn ...

His lies, His deceit
a new trap at every turn

The scales, they fell
from my eyes

And, I saw my Lord
take my place

I will not get
what I deserve

The gift
I did not earn

This favor
I can never return

The enemy
can not touch me

Though He wants to
watch me burn ...

A new snare
at every turn

The scales, they fell
from my eyes

The gift
I did not earn

I will not get
what I deserve

And He will not get to
watch me burn ...

THE MIREY CLAY

I think about the depths
From where I came
and I thank you Lord
you pulled me out of the mirey clay
and I am free
So now, I must not look back
I will keep my eyes on the prize
the chains, they fell from my hands and feet
you lifted me
and I am free
I will walk forward
and not look back
Everything has changed
and I became new

My love, and my hope grows
and each day, I am closer to you
and further from where I came
that day you pulled me out of the mirey clay
and I will not look back
My spirit is new because of you
you live in me
and everything has changed
I will keep my eyes on you
and no matter what
I will not look back
that is what I hear you say
Don't look back.

DEMONS INSIDE

Its spiritual warfare
the battle of the mind
when I search myself
the demons I find
they are trying to kill me
what must I do?
to conquer these demons
I must live in truth

Out of the darkness, into the light
can not give up, must continue to fight

All of the answers
I must search within
and to stop living a life full of sin

The battle of the mind
the demons inside

I call to my God
to Him, I confide

When will the insanity finally subside?
to stop living a life, that's a lie
to learn how to live
while their still is time

The battle within
but the choices are mine
to get busy living, or stay busy dying

And have victory
over the demons inside
I call to my God
to Him, I confide

NEVER ALONE

I'm surrounded by angels
I'm never alone.
As I take my walk
down this long, winding road.
and I feel I can't take another step
and they lift me, and carry me
so I can rest...
they give me hope, they give me strength
But, most of all, I'm never alone.
so I must stay on the narrow road.
because that is where my angels are
they remind me, I'm never alone.
when I come to another fork in the road.
to make a choice, to the left or the right
to know if I need to flee, or to fight
just to know that I'm never alone
along this journey
along this road
I'm surrounded by angels
I'm never alone

MICHAEL

I hear your footsteps
coming ever so closer
faster, louder
and my heart
step for step, beat for beat
I feel you breathe
at the nap of my neck
your odor, brings me to my knees
and your heat overpowers my breath
I cannot see, blackness is full
I know you by name
I try to escape, but you ensnare me
I no longer fight
my soul hangs by a thread
But, Michael comes
off with your head
your fluids drain to the ground
and melt everything around
But me
Michael lays me at the foot of the cross
I sob, and I live
I know you will return
stronger, meaner
But, so will Michael
For, you cannot have me - Ever

CHAPTER 3

WARFARE

Ephesians 6:12

For we wrestle not against flesh and blood but against principalities, against powers, against the rulers of the darkness of this world, against spiritual wickedness in high places.

KJV

WHEN IT WAS WRITTEN

IT IS FINISHED

The battle within is real
the Holy Spirit is at war
with my flesh -
and I lose plenty
of the battles,
but I will not lose the war -
I can not lose the war -
It was all nailed
to the cross -
and when He said:
IT IS FINISHED
- I won -

SCREAMS

When you ask me how I feel
and all I say is dumb.
Its hard for me to express myself
the depths from where I've come.
my mind screams, I am insane
see me now, what I became,
my heart is cold, my soul is stained.
and as I open up my mind,
manic chaos is what I find.
life is full, but death is near.
when I close my eyes, the screams I hear
and live this life fall of fear,
How much more can I bare?
to learn to love, and learn to care
and silence the screams within my head,
now its time, to love instead.

THIS NOISE

This noise in my head
will not let me sleep
some of my thoughts
go way too deep

That if I was to share
you'de say I was insane
and this noise in my head
causes nothing but pain

Why must I listen?
what must I do?
to open up
to tell you the truth

So what must I do
to silence this noise?
to have thoughts of love?
to have thoughts of joy?

I must find a way
to silence this noise.

This noise in my head
not reality,
this noise in my head
insanity.

It won't let me sleep
this noise in my head.
It won't let me rest
this noise wants me dead.

So what must I do
to silence this noise?
what must I do
to take back my mind?

So I won't be afraid
to close my eyes.
what must I do,
to take back my life?

I must find away
to silence this noise.

MENTAL MADNESS

I search myself, I search my mind
mental madness is what I find
I see myself, with all my sin
soul sickness, deep within
I feed myself, and then I grow
spiritual wickedness, cleanse my soul
the more I search, the better I feel
stop living a lie, start living what's real
to accept forgiveness, to accept love
to have faith in God above
mental madness, quiet this pain
I find myself, now I'm sane.

THE DRAGON

The dragon still lives, and waits
It waits, patiently
and breathes nothing but pain, and death
waiting for me to slip
so it can devour me
This is war
I am a soldier
and I must continue to fight the dragon
every day of my life
this is war
and the battlefield is my mind
my weapons are honesty, and kindness, and love
the dragon is larger than me
but my weapons are sufficient
if I keep them sharp, and polished
the dragon wants me dead
I must continue to fight
and in turn, I live.

RECLAIM YOUR SHAME

Watched you change
as you grew wings
the new you lives
as the old you dies
the old you tries
but the new you flies

Now your wings are torn
and your mind warped
watching you change
back to the old you
as you reclaim your shame

Its not too late
to grow new wings
the new you tries
but the old you thrives
as you reclaim your shame

BATTLE OF THE MIND

Your weapons from below
cannot penetrate
my armor from above
your weapons,
of hate, doubt, and fear
my armor
of love, faith, and strength
your weapons from below
my armor from above
I'm ready for you
I'm prepared for your kind
your weapons
my armor
the battle of the mind

CHAPTER 4

MASKS

Job 34:29b

And when he hideth his face
who then can behold him?

KJV

WHEN IT WAS WRITTEN

MY MASK

I put on a mask for every occasion
I hide myself, it is an illusion
I hide from me, I hide from you
you wouldn't love me, if you knew the truth
why must I use these masks? I'm confused
the times in the past, I've been battered and used
my heart, and my mind been scattered, and bruised
I hide from from the guilt, the hurt, and the pain
I hide from myself, I feel I'm insane
Now its time to take off my mask
to let you in, to take a chance
to open up, to take a glance
of who I am, what I became
stop living a lie, stop living in shame
to take off my mask, not be afraid

of all of the years, and all the tears
hid within, my doubts, my fears
I put on a smile, when I want to cry
afraid to live, afraid to die
afraid to love, afraid to try
now, its time to let you in
to take off my mask, its time to begin
to love myself, and start to forgive
all of the wrongs, all of my sin
all of my secrets, I try to keep
I close my eyes, but cannot sleep
some of the scars go way too deep
I'm tired of living alone, and lonely
now its time to show the real me
I take of my mask, now I am free

MASK OF PAIN

The pain I feel
the hate I breathe
this pain is real
this hate I seeth ...
the pain I hate
I hate the pain ...
the mask of pain
I wear is hate
I hate the mask
but it masks the pain ...

BELIEVE

I believe what you see
you can achieve

I believe what you speak
can become what you see

and what you give
is more important
than what you receive

and its even more important
that you truly believe
what you believe

DEEP WITHIN

Look at yourself, look deep within
see more than hair, bones, and skin
Find that beautiful person inside
and know that the lonely feelings subside

All of the years trying to fill the hole
the broken spirit, the lonely soul
But there is something
that I just have to say

Look at yourself, look deep within
all of your guilt, all of your sin
don't be afraid to show where you've been
only then, can your new life begin

All of the days, all of the years
all the frustrations, heartbreaks, and tears
all bottled up, sealed deep within
the things we've done, the places we've been

It all scars our heart
makes it callosed a thick
we must either share this
or else remain sick

All of the days, all of the years
all of our secrets, our hopes, and our fears
all bottled up, sealed deep within
we must open up, and let someone in

To give, and yes to receive love
after all, it is a gift from above
look at yourself, look deep within
are you comfortable in your own skin?

So there is one thing, that I know for sure
we must love ourselves, for love to endure
look at yourself look deep within
then only can your new life begin

THE WALL

I built up a wall between you and me
built up so high, I can't even see
the wall is so thick, I barely can breathe
I'm hiding from you, hiding from me
I look at myself, don't like what I see
and I think I can fix it, with a drug or a drink
the wall surrounds me, I can't even think
and now its time to tear down the wall
block by block, it crumbles, it falls
each block represents my defects, my flaws
Before I can walk, must learn how to crawl
Now I can see, now I can breathe.
I'm not afraid to let you see me
who I am, what's inside
this loneliness will finally subside
I never loved, I've never tried
a thousand tears, I know I've cried
now its time to dry my eyes
to tear down the wall, to let you inside

MY DISGUISE

I want to show you the real me
time to take off my disguise
to do this, I must face the truth
and look at myself in the eyes

What do I see when I search within?
who is that person inside?
Sometimes I feel like I wanna laugh
and sometimes I just wanna cry

I'm starting to feel some emotions
but my eyes they still are dry
I believe that this is all normal
when I decide to give it a try

At times, I'd rather not go there
But I have to
take off my disguise ...

CHAPTER 5

PAIN

Psalms 55:4a

My heart is sore, pained within me

KJV

WHEN IT WAS WRITTEN

FLAWED

Do not feel guilty
for being flawed.
You are not broken,
when you fall short.
No one is perfect,
their was only one ...
Even though you are not fragile,
be gentle with you
practice forgiveness...
you are not broken,
but only flawed
Do not be sorry for this ...
No one is perfect,
their was only one ...
you are not broken,
but only flawed ...

DROWNING

Sinking in my own misery
drowning in myself

Sinking so deep
drowning in my cell

Falling to my deepest depths
drowning in this hell

I think it's time to realize
I'm screaming out for help

Save me from this misery
Save me from myself

Save me from this dark, deep cell
pull me back from hell

I'm screaming through this misery
I'm drowning in this cell

THIS PAIN

Some of the pains in life
can be easily avoided
by the choices we make.

But what about the pain
that we cannot avoid?
What about the pain
that was caused by others?

And what about the pain
that was at the fault
of no one at all?
What do we do with this pain?

And then there is the pain
that resurfaces over time
that we thought
we had left behind

What is it that we
should do with this pain?

Some of the pains in life
can not be avoided.

What we do with this pain
is the question at hand.

The answer might be simply
just don't spread it.
This pain...

ADDICTED TO PAIN

Cry out, your going down
down into the trenches
will this pain ever cease?
You scream but no sound.

Do you want help,
or are you addicted to pain?
Are you looking for some relief?
You scream for help

But still no sound?
You are too deep
You are too far gone
Cry out, your going down

Down into the trenches
will this pain ever cease?
Do you want it to stop?
Or, are you addicted to pain?

DON'T CLOSE YOUR EYES

Don't close your eyes to the pain inside
everybody hurts, everybody cries.
We must learn to live this life
through the pain, through the strife.
Share who we are, all the pain inside.
Everybody hurts, everybody tries,
we only have so much time
your days are numbered, so are mine.
So don't close your eyes to the love inside.
Share it with others, now is the time.
Keep your eyes open, don't be blind
to all the wonderful things in this life.
Everybody hurts, everybody dies,
So let's make the best of it,
and don't close your eyes.

CHAINS OF PAIN

Break these chains that bind me
stop the pain that blinds me
the pain of chains around me
each steel link confines me
the pain inside denies me
these chains of pain surround me
now its time to find me
erase the tapes, rewind me
new hope inside defines me
freedoms mine - remind me

BURNT BRIDGES

I left a trail, I burned by bridges
through years, and years of bad decisions
relationships lost, bridges burnt
friendships lost, people hurt.
I lost myself along the way
should I leave, or should I stay?
And face this mess that I had made
face myself, not be afraid
there's got to be a better way
to learn to laugh, to learn to play
to ask forgiveness, to start today.
And build new bridges along the way
and find a way to break these chains
and stop living like I'm insane.
And face this mess that I had made
the time is now to start today.

CHAPTER 6

LIVING WATER

Proverbs 20:5a

Council in the heart of men
is like deep water

WHEN IT WAS WRITTEN

THE RIVERS EDGE

As I walk along the rivers edge ...
I notice Gods creations
the water trickling over the rocks, and
the wind blowing through the trees, and high grasses

I smell the fresh air
and the blooms of spring
and I am reminded, that God is at work.

So I sit on the bank of the rivers edge ...
and though the fish are not biting
I feel joyful, and content

I hear the laughter of young children
enjoying the day with grandpa
and it brings a smile to my face

The thoughts, and cares of the world
are left behind.
As I live in the moment
there, on the rivers edge ...

I feel the gentle breeze
and the sun warms my skin, and my heart

My joy, and peace is
shared with a passerby
as we connect in a subtle way, often unspoken

I believe the birds sing to God above
thanking Him, that their needs are met
and I inturn learn from them

So as I pack up to return home
I realize it is not about how many fish I caught

It is the connection with nature
the connection with God
the connection with others
who share the same space, and time

This was another successful day
there, on the rivers edge ...

IN MY HEAD

Guess how I'm feeling in my head?
No more fear, no more dread
I'm still alive, I should be dead
the things I've done
the things I've said
Its all still alive, in my head
remembering all the things you said
I felt you grow
the pain you fed
confusion, now its calm instead
I was alone, my heart, it bled
I'm still alive
you want me dead
Now, there's peace, in my head.

NOISE IN BETWEEN

Somethings strange
that I realized today

Its simple but,
its very deep

I can survive on silence
or deep conversation

But its the
noise inbetween

That makes me crazy...
can you relate?

THEREFORE, I WIN

I know what its like to be
judged on my appearance
as they roll their eyes
and shake their heads

But it helps me, not to judge
those who cross my path
and see they are exactly
where they are supposed to be
at this moment
So therefore, I win ...

I know what it is like to be
locked in a cage, and wait,
and hope that someone
will bring me the key

But it helps me to enjoy
my freedom, and to be able to
acknowledge what it is
to be truly free, and
so therefor, I win ...

I know what it is like to be doubted and to be
considered not good enough

But, it helps me to root
for the underdog, and to
search for the best in others
and to also help them
to see it in themselves, and
so therefore, I win...

I know what it is like to
be on the wrong side
of the tracks, where nobody
wants you to cross

But, it helps me to feel
everyones pain, and
so therefore, I win ...

I know what it is like to
accept me, and to love me
so therefore, I win ...

BALANCE

The sky may be cloudy
the day may be gray
I choose to see beauty
the tenderness of the flower pedal
though the root is strong
always two sides to every coin
its sometimes unclear
but balance seems fair
Times of pain easily forgotten
when joy surrounds us.
And all is fine
sometimes we give, and
other times we receive
love is always near
if we are willing
all is not lost
when we open our minds
anything is possible
and balance seems fair.

HIS TEARS

Even His tears were blood
He gave all, so that I could live
I saw the tool, that ripped His skin
He still saw love.
Because He saw Him, He looked above.
Looked to His left, He saw me
the pain, undescribable
they thrust His side
He could have stopped it all
But He saw me.
I was the reason He suffered that day
all of His fluids fell to the ground
red, and pink, there was no sound
Total darkness, there was no light
Even His tears were blood; that night
His head fell to the side
It is finished
He lived, He died
But His spirit lives forever
He lives in me
Because of Him, I live -

CHAPTER 7

LOVE

1 John 4:12b

If we love one another, God dwelleth
in us, and His love is perfected in us.

KJV

WHEN IT WAS WRITTEN

I -   Cheré, 2006

II -   When He Walked Up That Hill, 2006

III -   Never Met, 2020

IV -   Alone, 2010

V -   Nothing Without You, 2021

VI -   Love Someone, 2020

CHERÉ

I got a call, the other day
at first, I didn't know what to say
after all this time I've been away

It was someone whose very dear to me
and she made it very clear to me
that she loves me, and she misses me
she's my daughter Cheré ...

She called again, I could not believe
after all the times I lied, and deceived
the bond is still there
its easy to see

We'll plan a reunion
it will happen some day
this time I won't run
this time I'll stay

I love her, I miss her
she's my daughter Cheré ...

WHEN HE WALKED UP THAT HILL

When He walked up that hill
did He know how much
He would have to bleed?
When He walked up that hill
did He know me by name?
Would He have went if it was only me?

The pain He must have felt
the loneliness, unbearable
when He walked up that hill for me
He carried the very tree
the nails were driven for me

The shame that should have been mine
He took my shame that day

He is my Lord
He is my Savior
He is the Christ
I owe Him all
because He walked up that hill for me

He gave His all that day
there is nothing left to give

All His blood, every drop
He gave for me that day
when He walked up that hill

NEVER MET

How can I miss someone so much
that I have never met?
I know you are out there,
and when I find you
I will love you.
God is preparing me
For someone that I have never met
and when I find you
I will show you
How much I've missed you
Even though
we have never met ...

ALONE

A lonely life, a life without love
life without love is a lonely life
I must learn to love, and love to live
must learn how to receive, learn how to give
to stop always blaming, and start to forgive
to live to learn, and learn to live
to open up, to let you in
life without love is a lonely life
all of the hatred cuts like a knife
so now I know, that it is time
to let the loneliness subside
I must open up, and let you inside
I must learn to love, and love to live
to stop always taking, and learn how to give
only then, do I really live
If I do not love, I will surely die
So now I know, its time to try
to let the loneliness subside

NOTHING WITHOUT YOU

I'm nothing without you ...
you left so quickly
there was nothing I could do

I wish I could go back
to that day
I would do all I could
to try to make you stay

And I wish I had
the choice now
to show you

That I'm nothing
without you ...

LOVE SOMEONE

Why are you so sad?
don't be afraid to cry
Why are you alone?
don't be afraid to try

To love someone
and let someone love you

So don't close your eyes
to what's going on outside
don't close yourself in

Don't be so sad
and don't be afraid

To love someone
and let someone love you.

Printed in the United States
by Baker & Taylor Publisher Services